Ton. ........

# SOS

*Song of Songs*
*A fifty-day journey into the heart of God*

Library of Congress Catalogue-in-Publication Data is on file at the Library of Congress, Washington, DC.

ISBN 9781948754002

*To Darlene, Jason, Katie, Alison, Sal, Jennifer, and Rebecca*

# Table of Contents

# Acknowledgments

There are many I would like to thank for the completion of this project. The first I want to recognize is Jesus, the Christ. An encounter began this journey into His heart.

Thank you Jesus for the revelation of Your great love for me. For believing in me and my dreams. Pastor Bill Johnson for fathering me to spiritual health. Pastor Kris Vallotton for calling out my destiny. Though you two great men of God haven't said much to me personally, you lived greatness around me that called me to royalty. Thank you to Justin Stumvoll who stirred my heart to start this pursuit of one of my dreams. Seth Dahl for a friendship that loved me in some hard times…. You called me out to take another step. Carrie Lloyd for your encouragement in writing. Crystal Hart for actually believing that I could do this and kicked me into gear to get on it. Alison Garlinger one of my daughters for doing most of the initial typing. Kristy Evans for smiling, encouraging, and helping. Sherry, Tom, Bill, Scott, and many more I say thank you.

I would like to add a couple notes about my editor, Crystal Hart. This woman is a great woman. I remember the first time I saw her, and God said "You can trust her." And from the beginning of this project until now, I totally trusted her. She's a great mother, a great wife, a great friend. Very few people in my life have impacted me so, but in the moments that we've spent together, the presence of God was so real, we even had to stop a few times just to enjoy His presence. I look forward hopefully to more projects, but only after she gets some of her writing done, too. I'm honored to know her. I'm honored to know her family. And I know that Jesus walks with her everywhere she goes.

# Foreword

Over the many years of interpretation, the thousands if not millions of books that try to echo the true heart of the Lord, we could now easily complicate things. So much theology has, at times, skewered our understanding of His love for us. Christ, I believe came so that we may have life in abundance, because before then, we truly were complicating how to love God and how to understand His love for us. His incarnate arrival was perfect in timing, and when you look at Christ's teachings, His actions, His deeds, the brutal simplicity of the Songs of Songs, the passion in which God loves us really were reflected in His life.

I do wish I had been told earlier in my life just how much the presence of God would change our hearts and comfort us in the darkest times of my life. I believe I perhaps would not have left the church as a devout atheist after facing so much death in my family, and I could have held tighter to God's hand in those times. My identity was wrapped up in favour, over His comfort and yet fortunately, He hounded me and found me fed up of my own God-complex, I came back to Him, now as a firm believer, but it wasn't a logical decision, it was based on love.

This book gives a beautiful portrayal of just how brutally simple His love is for us. No conditions, no demands, no codependent bias, at least not from His side. And if we ever questioned His goodness as a reflection of what has happened in our own lives, then we fall short of all there is to offer in the passion of what was given to us in scripture thousands of years ago.

Tom has written pages dedicated to understanding just how passionate God's love is for us and as you unwind in each page, may these words not be another set of ideas that resolve some more theology, but may they be words that soak right into the very soul of the matter. May they heal wounds that tried to logistically fathom His kindness.

This book is a beautiful companion for times in the secret place, times to look at His perspective on whatever you may be facing right now. To finally understand our identity based on how He loves us, and what better way to discover that, than reading the most romantic book in the Bible?

I pray as you delve into each thought, that you may be beautifully romanced by Him and that your heart finally finds its home.

—Pastor Carrie Lloyd, author of *Virgin Monologues* and *Prude*

# Preface

This book is designed to be a 2-10 minute guided time with the Lord with prayer prompts and space provided to write down your thoughts and feelings from the Lord during your time with Him as He pours His rich love into you.

It is He who loves me…. And it is He who really loves you, as well. Whether you are man or woman and no matter what we go through in our lives His love for us will never change and nothing will ever separate us from His love, Romans 8. Jesus not only loves us but He is deeply in love with us. "Lord, who fully knows power of your passion and the intensity of your emotions?" (Psalm 90:11, *TPT*). This is the essence of what this book is about: His deep love.

The next few weeks as you enter into the very arms of Jesus, if you choose, the Master Craftsman will Champion and mold you more into His image. God is deeply in love with us, passionately pursuing you and beckons you to come away with Him. Though the end result to each destiny may look different, we are all on a journey. Your journey will look quite different than mine but He takes pleasure and dances with us along the way.

God is good. He loves you, and this love creates the platform of identity for your life. But what you are willing to give and commit, He will be faithful to transform your life.

My prayer is that as you dive in, you will abandon your heart to God and realize that He is in love with you. He is preparing you and has given everything you could ever need to be His bride. As a man, I know we can have a difficult hard time understanding the concept of being a bride, but if you are a man, I wholly invite you, too, to come with me on this adventure of discovery. I bless you on this journey as you watch your heart be molded into His and let your life be transformed.

As you embark on this journey I can't emphasize enough to be honest with yourself and God—we can't fool Him anyway. The questions to answer are there for reflection and there are no wrong answers. Be free to answer as what you know as truth inside you; honestly ask and write the first thing that comes into your mind. As long as it is consistent with the Bible and is born out of love and for the purpose of healing, write it down. I have found that any thought that is encouraging, edifying, and comforting normally comes from God.

Consistency is so important to maintaining relationship with Jesus. A plant that is not kept up will eventually choke from weeds or die from lack of nutrition. A personal relationship can't grow without consistent communication. So it is with our spirit. The more we are aware of the heart of God daily, moment by moment, the more we are "watered" by Him. His presence is always around you.

I strongly encourage you obtain a copy of The Passion Translation of Song of Songs, but it's not necessary as I provide the passages in the book.

Pray this with me:

Holy Spirit, I thank You for Your presence and I acknowledge You are here now. You are free to speak as You desire and pour Your love into me as I use this devotional. I take every thought captive to You. Thank You for this time and the time I take every day to meditate on You and Your Word. Jesus, thank You for purchasing me with Your blood and making me a son/daughter of the Father. You have made me from my mother's womb for a destiny that You wrote in Your Book. I give my all to You and thank You for giving Your all for me. Thank You for loving me and desiring to draw close to me. Amen.

# Day 1

## SOS 1:2, *TPT*

*The Shulamite:*
*"Let him smother me with kisses—his Spirit-kiss divine. So*
*kind are your caresses, I drink them in like the sweetest wine!"*

God is always, in every way, good—no exception. He's not angry with anyone; rather, he desires to be intimate with everyone.

The enemy of our souls deliberately tries to destroy our intimacy. "The thief does not come except to steal, and to kill, and to destroy. I have come that they may have life, and that they may have it more abundantly" (John 10:10, *NKJV*). Jesus longs to bring abundant life into your very being with the same kiss that brought life to Adam. It's the Word of God that kisses your mouth, breathing life into you. "Death and life are in the power of the tongue, and those who love it will eat its fruit" (Proverbs 18:21, *NKJV*).

Our soul's cry is this: "I want to be smothered by Your love, Your Word, and Your life. Jesus, all I want is You. Nothing else will ever satisfy."

This is the most intimate request we could ever ask…for the Maker of the universe to come and manifest His love to us. As he kisses you, His breathes life into you and you are now alive in Him. He is breathing into you the revelation of His love for you. Your spirit opens up to the realization that God is not some distant, impersonal love that looks to punish you. He deeply, deeply loves you! All your value is wrapped up in what He paid to purchase your freedom, the life of Jesus, his son, to set you free.

You are worth it!

It can seem like we're the only ones desiring His kiss, His intimacy, He also longs for our kiss as well. He longs to reach out his hands, cup your face, and stare deeply, lovingly into your eyes and breathe life into you. We bless him by openly turning our affection to Him. Kisses in nature are open and vulnerable, and this is how we enter into his presence—nothing hidden. God desires to be so intimate with us, may I say, even vulnerable. Be uninhibited and kiss Him.

The Hebrew word for kiss, *nashaq* in Song of Songs, can also mean to arm or equip for battle. He kisses us, fills us with his love, and that personal touch empowers and equips us to meet our day as conquerors, champions.

We don't live out of obligation or compulsion, rather, from a platform love, the sure knowledge that we are beloved "children of God" (Romans 8:16, *NKJV*). What I do, I do out of love for my Beloved…and He does out of love for His bride.

"Father, thank you for your love. What do you love most about me today?"

_____
_____
_____
_____
_____
_____
_____
_____
_____
_____
_____
_____
_____
_____
_____
_____
_____
_____
_____
_____
_____
_____
_____
_____
_____
_____
_____
_____
_____
_____

# Day 2

SOS 1:3, *TPT*

*The Shulamite:*
*"Your presence releases a fragrance so pleasing—over and over*
*poured out. For your lovely name is 'Flowing Oil.' No wonder*
*the brides-to-be adore you."*

The presence of the Lord releases a fragrance, the fragrance of heaven, the fragrance of freedom, the fragrance of new life.

While lying on the floor preparing to speak at a church, the presence of the Holy Spirit fell and I smelled the tangible fragrance of God as a rich combination of sweet smelling oils. His presence releases an actual fragrance that's so pleasing. He is so generous; He continues to pour it out on us over and over, never stopping until we ask.

There is no denying when His presence enters a room. Remember the woman that broke the alabaster box and poured the oil out on Jesus' feet in John 12. The fragrance was so strong that it affected everyone in the whole room. A strong scent has a way of filling every place it enters.

Even His name behaves as "Flowing Oil." His name covers and consumes and is not a stagnant word, but flows, running into every crack and groove until it captivates our entire beings. Picture a waterfall, not of water, but of oil, a never-ending, fragrant stream of healing, anointing, and refreshment. He pursues you. He envelops you in His presence and permeates you with His love.

"Father, thank you for Your presence, your Flowing Oil. What does it mean for me to be consumed by You, to have every part of me filled by Your pleasing fragrance?"

# Day 3

*The Shulamite:*
*"Draw me into your heart. We will run away together into the*
*king's cloud-filled chamber."*

My heart cries out to be drawn into the very heart of God, to be drawn so deep into Him that no one can tell where He ends and I begin.

James 4:8 tells us to draw near to Him and He will draw near to us. And Proverbs 18:10 says that He is our refuge, "The name of the Lord is a strong tower; the righteous run into it and are safe" (*NKJV*).

We can never be in a position to be led until we find ourselves hidden in Him. When we are hidden, everything we do is born from connection and relationship. From this intimacy, we run away together into His cloud-filled chamber, a picture of Holy Spirit taking us into the holy of holies inside the temple chamber. In this chamber of the King of Kings, I can now have intimate access with the Creator of the entire universe. His blood allows us bold access into His heart, as stated in Hebrews 4:16, "So now we come freely and boldly to where love is enthroned, to receive mercy's kiss and discover the grace we urgently need to strengthen us in our time of weakness" (*TPT*).

The cloud-filled chamber gives a tangible picture of the very presence of God. His cloud that filled the temple in Solomon's time is the same as in the tabernacle in Moses time when no one could stand but shouted in joy over the visitation of God. Our secret place is found in the cloud-filled chamber and He welcomes us in.

"God, take me into Your holy of holies. Let me see Your face, Your glory, Your love. I fall on my face before You and worship You."

Write down your experience.

_____

_____

_____

_____

_____

_____

_____

_____

_____

_____

_____

_____

_____

_____

_____

_____

_____

_____

_____

_____

_____

_____

_____

_____

_____

_____

_____

_____

_____

_____

_____

_____

_____

_____

_____

# Day 4

## SOS 1:5-6, *TPT*

*The Shulamite:*
*"Jerusalem maidens, in this twilight darkness*
*I know I am so unworthy—so in need."*
*The Shepherd-King:*
*"Yet you are so lovely!"*
*The Shulamite:*
*"I feel as dark and dry as the desert tents of the wandering*
*nomads."*
*The Shepherd-King:*
*"Yet you are so lovely—like the fine linen tapestry hanging in*
*the Holy Place."*
*The Shulamite to Her Friends:*
*"Please don't stare in scorn because of my dark and sinful ways.*
*My angry brothers quarreled with me and appointed me*
*guardian of their ministry vineyards, yet I've not tended my*
*vineyard within."*

Many times I've fallen into the trap of seeing myself different than Jesus sees me, unworthy, dirty, empty, moody, or a mess. But God sees me as lovely, beautiful, and whole. Just like the tapestry that hangs around the holy of holies, around the mercy seat and beautifies it; so do we beautify the most holy place. The tapestry veil that was created by an anointed craftsman was never intended to separate but to beautify.

We are designed to beautify every atmosphere we are in and draw people to the God that loves them and does not desire to separate them though religious ways, as in Romans 8:15: "For you did not receive the spirit of bondage again to fear, but you received the Spirit of adoption by whom we cry out, 'Abba, Father'" (*NKJV*).

In the beginning Jesus said that no one could see His face and live. Yet He always wanted us in relationship, wanted us to behold His beauty. When we receive Jesus we die; it is no longer I who lives but Jesus lives in me as in Galatians 2:20a: "I have been crucified with Christ; it is no longer I who live but Christ who lives in me" (*NKJV*). And since I am dead, so to speak, I can see His face.

When Jesus tore the veil, He tore the oppression of man and poured His blood over the mercy seat. Now we can boldly come to Him because we belong. Because of His blood we are now beautified.

"Reveal the truth about me. You say I am lovely. Show me."

# Day 5

## SOS 1:7, *TPT*

*The Shulamite:*
*"Won't you tell me, lover of my soul, where do you feed your*
*flock? Where do you lead your beloved ones to rest in the heat of*
*the day? For I wish to be wrapped all around you as I wander*
*among the flocks of your shepherds. It is you I long for, with no*
*veil between us!"*

The question the Shulamite asks is addressed to "the lover of my soul." It is the proper name, attitude, and heart of God our Father, Jesus, and Holy Spirit. He is the Lover of my soul. He is not controlling. No, He sets you free! He is not unrighteous in judging nor is He mean; He is joy, righteous, love, and peace. He has no chaos, rather, He holds all things together. This kind of peace is what Shalom means. All was created by Him, for Him, and from Him.

When I ask, "Where do you lead your beloved ones?" the question implies that I want to get there, too. "Where do You feed your flock? Where do you lead the beloved?" Take me there. Take me in out of the heat of the day, into rest. When heat comes in full force, that is not the time to do excessive work or strain. Rather, it is a time for Sabbath rest. We long to be enveloped by Him with His arms wrapped around us. Our sole desire is to be with Him in undivided, pure, unblemished intimacy. We want to be totally vulnerable with Him, open and unhidden. But really, can we hide anything from Him?

.

"Where You feed them, You also want to feed me. Reveal this place and take me there."

_____
_____
_____
_____
_____
_____
_____
_____
_____
_____
_____
_____
_____
_____
_____
_____
_____
_____
_____
_____
_____
_____
_____
_____
_____
_____
_____
_____
_____

# Day 6

*The Shepherd-King:*
*"Listen, my radiant one—if you ever lose sight of me, just follow*
*in my footsteps where I lead my lovers. Come with your burdens*
*and cares. Come to the place near the sanctuary of my*
*shepherds."*

God says, "If you ever lose sight of Me, follow in My footsteps." That is where He leads His lovers. I can lose my step or get off the path and sometimes a simple adjustment is all I needed to get back on track.

Come back into His footsteps, His footprints. Search what He is like and do those things. What would the Father do? That's all Jesus did. He only did what he saw the Father do, and He lived as our example. Jesus often went to the mountain to talk to the Father, and waited until He was commissioned to do those things.

Jesus had a custom to go to the mountain to pray. We don't all have access to retreat to the mountains, but we can find somewhere alone and quite, perhaps even in our minds like a garden bench or a quiet attic space. We all need somewhere to go to meet Him. He is eagerly waiting there for us.

"Are you weary, carrying a heavy burden? Then come to me. I will refresh your life, for I am your oasis" (Matthew 11:28, (*TPT*). Come to the place of safety, in pasture protected by His shepherds. There you find Him. You can carry on in His presence no matter what you do. Working, playing, sleeping, His presence can always be in your midst.

"Father, I give You my burdens. Refresh my life. Give me eyes to see as You see. Show me one area that needs to be invaded by your love."

After, hold out your hands and receive.

# Day 7

SOS 1:9, *TPT*

*The Shepherd-King:*
*"My dearest one, let me tell you how I see you—you are so*
*thrilling to me. To gaze upon you is like looking at one of*
*Pharaoh's finest horses—a strong, regal steed pulling his royal*
*chariot."*

God is saying to you, "Let me tell you how I see you. You are so thrilling to Me." Wow! I thrill God. You thrill God! He calls you "my dearest one."

Can there any doubt now or any question how God thinks of you? No one can ever put into words or properly identify the depth of His love. No one can come close to describing the amount of love He shows us on a daily basis. You stir His senses deeply that He is overcome by you. You are thrilling to Him. God desires your nearness even more than you desire His!

Pharaoh's finest horses were trained to perfection, to know the slightest touch or command—they knew what the master wanted and obeyed. They were the most beautiful, desired, well-bred, cherished, cared for, willing horses that existed. This is how God sees you.

Speak it out loud now, as many times as you need.

"I thrill God." Let this settle into your spirit. "I thrill God." All of you thrills Him. "I thrill God." You don't disappoint Him. "I thrill God." You are amazing in His eyes. "I thrill God." He cares more about your tomorrow and your dreams than even you do. "I thrill God." He is passionate for you. Just one look from you undoes Him. "I thrill the Lover of my soul."

Listen. He is speaking to you now. He is thrilled with you and wants to tell you personally.

_____
_____
_____
_____
_____
_____
_____
_____
_____
_____
_____
_____
_____
_____
_____
_____
_____
_____
_____
_____
_____
_____
_____
_____
_____
_____
_____
_____
_____
_____
_____

# Day 8

## SOS 1:11, *TPT*

*The Shepherd-King:*
*"We will enhance your beauty, encircling you with our golden*
*reins of love. You will be marked with our redeeming grace."*

The Father, Son and Holy Spirit mark us, brand us, set us apart with grace that rescues, delivers, and atones for wrongs. He redeemed us when we didn't deserve redemption. Romans 5:8 says, "But God demonstrates His own love toward us, in that while we were still sinners, Christ died for us" (*NKJV*). Jesus, the lover of our soul, died for us when we were in our worst state and paid the most expensive price to bring us into our destiny.

The Shepherd-King says, "We will enhance your beauty." We, being the Trinity, have created us, are still creating us. He desires to make us more beautiful. We are adorned with golden reigns and marked in redemption. Since documented in Genesis 1:26a, He has His hand in every aspect of us as individuals: "Let us make man in Our image" (*NKJV*). You are made in God's image—*God's* image—beautiful in every aspect. He adorns you and removes all that is not from Him. People have placed things on you that do not match who you are. God is shredding those false ornaments and is personally adorning you with gold.

Father, Son, Holy Spirit put their hands in and take this clay of us to form it so every place we step is beautified. His grace redeems us. God is in the business of restoration, the kind that makes all things new, not just a fixed up version, but excellent. You are excellent.

Redemption entails filling in the blanks of all we missed or had stolen from us. He redeems *time, items,* and the internal *stuff* and makes us brand new. "Therefore, if anyone is in Christ, he is a new creation; old things have passed away; behold, all things have become new" (2 Corinthians 5:17, *NKJV*). Paul is clear that the old is passed away, dead, no longer alive—and the new has come, the new you. According to Isaiah 43:18-19, we're not to meditate on things from the past; He is doing a new thing and now it will spring forth! He even promises to "make a road in the wilderness and rivers in the desert" (*NKJV*).

The Trinity has marked you, put a label on you of redeeming grace. You permanently have the "immunity idol" of redemption; you won't be voted off like in Survivor. But even better, grace defines you, renews you, and beautifies you.

"My Lord, how has grace made me new and beautified me?"

_____

_____

_____

_____

_____

_____

_____

_____

_____

_____

_____

_____

_____

_____

_____

_____

_____

_____

_____

_____

_____

_____

_____

_____

_____

_____

_____

_____

_____

_____

_____

_____

_____

_____

_____

_____

# Day 9

SOS 1:12-14, *TPT*

*The Shulamite:*
*"As the king surrounded me at his table, the sweet fragrance of*
*my praise perfume awakened the night.*
*"A sachet of myrrh is my lover, like a tied-up bundle of myrrh*
*resting over my heart.*
*"He is like a bouquet of henna blossoms—henna plucked near*
*the vines at the fountain of the Lamb. I will hold him and never*
*let him part."*

"The king surrounded me . . . the sweet fragrance of my praise perfume awakened the night" (Song of Songs 1:12, *TPT*). The King, like Boaz covering Ruth with a blanket, covers and surrounds us with His deepest love. We are totally enveloped by His arms—by His sheltering wings proving safety and security.

My praise is a sweet perfume to God's nose. Perfume has a way of permeating everything around. Our praise permeates any place we may be. It fills the very atmosphere until everything and everyone around us is affected by the fragrance of praise. And all in the night are awakened; no one can sleep or be comatose when the sweet aroma of praise fills the room.

The myrrh is over our hearts—a beautiful picture of the cross that bought us and redeemed us, and now rests upon us. Henna and the fountain of the Lamb represent atonement, re-emphasizing redeeming grace. Henna comes from the root word for "ransom price" or "redemption." Myrrh is also fragrant, an unmistakable rich scent, emitting proof of our salvation and ongoing beautification.

"My praise is a sweet fragrance to You." Take a minute to offer Him thankful praise.

"Father, how does my praise affect Your heart?"

_____

_____

_____

_____

_____

_____

_____

_____

_____

_____

_____

_____

_____

_____

_____

_____

_____

_____

_____

_____

_____

_____

_____

_____

_____

_____

_____

_____

_____

_____

_____

_____

# Day 10

SOS 1:15, *TPT*

*The Shepherd-King:*
*"Look at you, my dearest darling, you are so lovely! You are*
*beauty itself to me. Your passionate eyes are like gentle doves."*

Take a look at yourself. Most of the time, we see ourselves through the eyes of the accuser of the brethren, either by labels others have placed on us—lies spoken against who we really are—or through a low self-image.

God sees you through the precious blood Jesus shed for you. Those who come into His arms and receive Him are so extraordinarily lovely in His eyes.

Take a look at yourself again, this time through His eyes. To see you as God sees you is transformation; it is the renewing of your mind. You—yes, you—are the epitome of beauty, the very incarnation of beauty—beauty personified.

Your eyes show what's inside your heart like little, revelatory portals. "Your passionate eyes are like gentle doves." In passion you burn for the Holy Spirit, symbolized as a dove, Who is gentle, sensitive, and powerful. What a great combination—passion and power. You keep our eyes on the Holy Spirit and live out what you see, dependent on Him. You look like His peace when even in the midst of chaos, you live in His gentle yet powerful, love-filled atmosphere.

Picture being face to face with Jesus or Father, close enough to look deeply into His eyes, and He into yours.

Ask Him, "How do you see me?"

# Day 11

## SOS 2:1, *TPT*

*The Shulamite:*
*"I am truly his rose, the very theme of his song. I'm*
*overshadowed by his love, growing in the valley!"*

I am His rose! The root word in Hebrew, *habab,* is the same word as the one used in Genesis 1:2 when His Spirit hovered over the surface of the deep—overshadowed. He overshadows me, broods over me, hovers over me. As Mary was overshadowed when Holy Spirit planted in her the seed of Jesus, He plants Jesus' spirit in us so that in all we do we birth Him. We are no longer orphans; we are no longer widows. We are sons, daughters, and brides of the Creator of the universe. We no longer need to fend for ourselves. We are in the care of the One Who sings over us.

The Rose of Sharon—you are under the canopy of His love, overshadowed by the One Who sings over you.

The valley is an amazing place to grow. Fed by the water that runs down from the mountains, protected from harsh winds—it's a place life can flourish and multiply.

"Lord, what are the words to the song you sing over me?"

# Day 12

SOS 2:2, *TPT*

*The Shepherd-King:*
*"Yes, you are my darling companion. You stand out from all*
*the rest. For though the curse of sin surrounds you, still you*
*remain as pure as a lily, even more than all others."*

Darling means dearly loved. Many of us never realize that we are dearly loved. Often, we know God loves us because His Word says so, but not to the extent that we are *dearly* loved, *deeply* loved. Being dearly loved solidifies the truth of us as the ones that make His heart beat, make His blood rush, that thrill Him. We stir Him in passion.

You stand out from the rest. While the results of sin are all around you, He sees you as pure—more than others. Paraphrased from Isaiah 1:18, your sins were red as scarlet, now you are white as fresh snow. Because of the blood of Jesus, you are made clean, pure, and righteous. You were born into sin. When you gave your life to Him, you died—the sinner part died and you were resurrected with Christ. Referring back to Galatians 2:20 again, "It is no longer I who lives but Christ lives in me" (*NKJV*). You carry His DNA. You might sin, but it is not who you are, and sin no longer has power over you. It died.

You've been given His nature—Jesus' nature, His DNA inside you. You radiate beauty, purity, Him, every place you go.

You are God's favorite. You are not only loved; you are *dearly* loved.

"God, open my eyes to see and experience this incredible love you have for me."

_____

_____

_____

_____

_____

_____

_____

_____

_____

_____

_____

_____

_____

_____

_____

_____

_____

_____

_____

_____

_____

_____

_____

_____

_____

_____

_____

_____

_____

_____

_____

_____

# Day 13

## SOS 2:3-6, *TPT*

*The Shulamite:*
*"My beloved is to me the most fragrant apple tree—he stands above the sons of men. Sitting under his grace-shadow, I blossom in his shade, enjoying the sweet taste of his pleasant, delicious fruit, resting with delight where his glory never fades.*
*"Suddenly, he transported me into his house of wine—he looked upon me with his unrelenting love divine.*
*"Revive me with your raisin cakes. Refresh me again with your apples. Help me and hold me, for I am lovesick! I am longing for more—yet how could I take more?*
*"His left hand cradles my head while his right hand holds me close. I am at rest in this love."*

Revive me, refresh me, I am at rest and I long for more of You, God! "Oh, taste and see that the Lord is good" (Psalm 34:8a, *NKJV*). Drink deeply of the pleasures of God. He is so good! Better than we think. Think of peaceful days, the most delicious food baking in the oven, the rich aroma filling the whole house—hunger is awakened. We want to taste and discover how the delicious source of the scent and as we eat, sustenance filters through our entire bodies, bringing nutrients to every fiber of our being, bringing us refreshment and life.

Imagine a sailboat stalled out in the middle of a lake, waiting in the dead calm for a wind. No ripples in the water, the sails hang slack, when suddenly, a light zephyr breathes life into the sail, increasing intensity until the fabric stretches to full capacity and the boat speeds through the water. His refreshing wind blows life into our souls.

Let Holy Spirit fill your soul, like a cold rain on a hot day, and suddenly you have vitality and vibrancy again. Now you are full and begin to cry out, "I want more!"

"I'm longing for more—yet how could I take more?" This is like Thanksgiving, when you are so full, but the desert looks and smells so amazing that you want more. God is so glorious and good that when we taste, we can't help but want more even when we are so satisfied. The closer we get in Him the better He tastes and the hungrier we get. "I am at rest in this love."

Taste and see that the Lord is good!
"More. I want more, of you. Overflow me."

# Day 14

## SOS 2:8, *TPT*

*The Shulamite:*
*"Listen! I hear my lover's voice. I know it's him coming to*
*me—leaping with joy over mountains, skipping in love over the*
*hills that separate us, to come to me."*

We recognize His voice. Jesus said, "My sheep hear my voice and I know them" (John 10:27a, *NKJV*). Sheep know their Shepherd's voice, and we are His sheep. He knows us intimately, knows our every thought, every heartbeat.

He is my lover—the lover of my soul. Think of the person you love most. First you catch the sound of that person's voice, the sound of footsteps, the familiar scent. All your senses are heightened, your heartbeat speeds up, and the butterflies of excitement fill your stomach—the love of your life has just entered the room. You know it's Him. You can always sense when the one you love and loves you is near. The choice is whether or not you respond.

He is coming to you. He is in passionate pursuit of you. He's coming—running, ready to crash down over you like a wave in a storm surging on the ocean, encompassing you. You lose control, yet you are free as His love envelopes you.

Psalm 139:17-18 speaks of God's loving thoughts of us are more numerous than the grains of sand on all the shores.

"Father, what are several loving thoughts You have toward me?"

_____
_____
_____
_____
_____
_____
_____
_____
_____
_____
_____
_____
_____
_____
_____
_____
_____
_____
_____
_____
_____
_____
_____
_____
_____
_____
_____
_____
_____
_____

# Day 15

SOS 2:9, *TPT*

*The Shulamite:*
*"Let me describe him: he is graceful as a gazelle, swift as a wild*
*stag. Now he comes closer, even to the places where I hide. He*
*gazes into my soul, peering through the portal as he blossoms*
*within my heart."*

David said in Psalm 139:7-8, "Where can I go from Your presence . . . behold You are there" (*NKJV*).

We can't hide from Him—not a thought, desire, or want. As He comes to meet with us in the cool of the day, He calls out, so deeply desiring to fellowship with us as He did with Adam in the garden. He always comes closer, pursuing us like He did with the woman at the well, with quietly calling Matthew, with Mary and Martha. He desires relationship—fellowship. And all He's doing is quietly calling us to come follow Him.

He peers into our souls, the very places where we are real and devoid of pretensions. It is here we become vulnerable with God, opening our hearts to Him, and He in turn becomes vulnerable with us. And it's in this place as He gazes into our souls, that He blossoms within our hearts, revealing Himself to us.

When blossoms open, they release a rich fragrance; when He is close, He blossoms within us and His fragrance permeates every atmosphere we enter. He desires to be so close to us that no one would be able to tell us apart.

41

"Father, I am here, eyes wide open, nothing hidden. Look into my eyes, gaze deeply in my soul, so my heart will expand to overflowing with Your great love for me."

# Day 16

SOS 2:10–13a, *TPT*

*The Bridegroom-King:*
*"Arise, my dearest. Hurry, my darling. Come away with me! I have come as you have asked to draw you to my heart and lead you out. For now is the time, my beautiful one.*
*"The season has changed, the bondage of your barren winter has ended, and the season of hiding is over and gone. The rains have soaked the earth,*
*"and left it bright with blossoming flowers. The season for singing and pruning the vines has arrived. I hear the cooing of doves in our land, filling the air with songs to awaken you and guide you forth.*
*"Can you not discern this new day of destiny breaking forth around you? The early signs of my purposes and plans are bursting forth. The budding vines of new life are now blooming everywhere. The fragrance of their flowers whispers, 'There is change in the air . . .'"*

This is the season for singing, bright with blossoming flowers! The wooing of Holy Spirit awakens and guides us into the new day of destiny, into His plans and purposes.

The earth soaks up the rain leaves the ground bright with blossoming flowers; we are the earth soaking up the Holy Spirit. He drenches us so we're beautified and overcome our world with the aroma of heaven.

The Bridegroom-King can hardly wait to be with his bride. "Arise, shine; for your light has come!" (Isaiah 60:1a, *NKJV*). He burns with passion for you and me. Now is the time to arise and take our places as sons and daughters of the kingdom of heaven, as brides of Jesus. Today starts a new season. The old has passed away; the new has come. Our barrenness is over.

Now, He has opened up our wombs to bear fruit, our soil to grow fresh seeds full of life. The protective seed-shell we put around ourselves is gone, decomposing while we rise up as fresh tender shoots, sincere and unguarded with Him. Rains have soaked the earth; the torrential downpour of the Holy Spirit has come. And like little seeds, we want more! We want to soak in more until we can't take anymore and then we cry out for more.

"God I want more of you! What does this season of spring look like in my life?"

_____
_____
_____
_____
_____
_____
_____
_____
_____
_____
_____
_____
_____
_____
_____
_____
_____
_____
_____
_____
_____
_____
_____
_____
_____
_____
_____
_____
_____
_____
_____
_____

# Day 17

SOS 2:13b-14, *TPT*

*The Bridegroom-King:*
*". . . Arise, my love, my beautiful companion, and run with me*
*to the higher place. For now is the time to arise and come away*
*with me.*
*"For you are my dove, hidden in the split-open rock. It was I*
*who took you and hid you up high in the secret stairway of the*
*sky. Let me see your radiant face and hear your sweet voice.*
*How beautiful your eyes of worship and lovely your voice in*
*prayer."*

Run to the higher place; arise and come away! Let Him see your radiant face, your beautiful eyes of worship, and your lovely voice of prayer. Catch those foxes that raid and try to ruin your budding love-vineyard that He has planted within you.

Don't wait to get to that higher place. Coming up higher changes our perception of people, circumstances, and everything else in our lives. Up here, we can actually see the whole forest, rather than the few trees around us, like the saying, "You can't see the forest for the trees." Up here, everything becomes clear. We may not always see the paths to take, but here, we can more easily trust Him to make a way.

When we come away with him, He becomes our focus, our passion, our praise, our everything. And He is overcome by the beauty of our eyes of worship, by the loveliness of our voice in prayer, by simply meeting us as we pray. What intimacy this brings! He loves and craves conversation with us, the private time where we can be vulnerable with each other—where we can be wholly known and accepted just as we are.

"Lord, I turn all my focus on You and let cares of everything else in my life disappear. Give me new perspective. Let me see everything around me through Your eyes."

# Day 18

## SOS 2:16-17, *TPT*

*The Shulamite:*
*"I know my lover is mine and I have everything in you, for we
delight ourselves in each other.*
*"But until the day springs to life and the shifting shadows of fear
disappear, turn around, my lover, and ascend to the holy
mountains of separation without me. Until the new day fully
dawns, run on ahead like the graceful gazelle and skip like the
young stag over the mountains of separation. Go on ahead to the
mountain of spices—I'll come away another time."*

We have everything in Him. But waiting until the shadows
of fear disappear is like trying to get clean before taking a shower.
Jesus cleans us from our filthy state. As mentioned in Romans 5:8,
we were sinners when Jesus chose to die to cleanse us. We truly
have everything in Him already, yet we often feel like we can't be
in relationship with Him until we are "whole" emotionally,
physically, and spiritually. That feeling is born from the poverty
mentality. We do not need to wait. We can jump into relationship
with Him right away. He longs for relationship, for making us
whole.

Vulnerability is the key to true freedom and intimacy with
Jesus. In this passage, we delight ourselves in Him, but we are not
yet vulnerable with Him. There is risk in vulnerability, in staying
openhearted, physically and emotionally. It can be scary, but well
worth the moments with Him. He won't ever harm you; He will
make you whole.

Though the Shulamite says she will come away another
time, we can't afford to wait. Don't let the wooing pass. He has
already called us away to come and join Him. Don't delay. Come
away now.

"What am I still holding onto? What keeps me from more intimacy and going deeper into your love?" As He reveals this, give it all to Him and soak up His presence.

_____
_____
_____
_____
_____
_____
_____
_____
_____
_____
_____
_____
_____
_____
_____
_____
_____
_____
_____
_____
_____
_____
_____
_____
_____
_____
_____
_____
_____
_____
_____

# Day 19

## SOS 3:1-3, *TPT*

*The Shulamite:*
*"Night after night I'm tossing and turning on my bed of travail.*
*Why did I let him go from me? How my heart now aches for*
*him, but he is nowhere to be found!*
*"So I must rise in search of him, looking throughout the city,*
*seeking until I find him. Even if I have to roam through every*
*street, nothing will keep me from my search. Where is he—my*
*soul's true love? He is nowhere to be found.*
*"Then I encountered the overseers as they encircled the city. So I*
*asked them, "Have you found him—my heart's true love?"*

My heart aches with longing for Him.

When we delay in responding to His wooing or His drawing us closer our hearts start to ache for His loving encounter. The ache is the catalyst that draws us into pursuit of Him. The question always is, "Why did we let Him go?" Finding the answer to that question can help us to not let Him go again. Don't let regret ensnare you, it's a trap of the enemy to separate you from His love.

The Shulamite goes out and searches everywhere, not caring how long or arduous the task. She goes to get him, no matter the cost to herself.

The overseers you encounter may not have that same desire or passion you do. They might not know the answer or be willing to help you search. Go to the Word. Go to Him. Embrace Him. Someone once said if you are looking for a prophetic word you should go to the Bible and read it. There are plenty of passages. He rewards those who diligently seek Him—He is the reward. And as we pursue His love, it becomes deeper, stronger, and more powerful than we can imagine.

"Jesus, where are you in this season in my life?"

# Day 20

SOS 3:4, *TPT*

*The Shulamite:*
*"Just as I moved past them, (the overseers) I encountered him. I*
*found the one I adore! I caught him and fastened myself to him,*
*refusing to be feeble in my heart again. Now I'll bring him back*
*to the temple within where I was given new birth—into my*
*innermost parts, the place of my conceiving."*

The daily exercise in the life of any believer is to invite Him deep into our very most depths of being, the depths of who we are, the place where "I am." The great I Am dwells in that place of who I am, puts me on as a cloak, and then lives in me. I no longer live, but Christ lives in me.

"Just as I moved passed them, I encountered Him." I fastened myself to Him. Get past the people, the distractions, move past man's shackles, and find Him. Embrace Him and become His cloak.

Sometimes people, some well-meaning or not, distract us from our ultimate goal which is Him. Then there are those who point us in the right direction; God puts those He trusts in our path to guide us to Him. They are few in number, and are recognizable because they do not seek to control or make us do what we should. Rather, they encourage, stir, and push us forward.

Encountering Him is not a chance meeting. Rather, it's a time of intimate fellowship and communion. We are coming into the embrace of our heavenly Lover who gave His life to purchase our redemption. We fasten ourselves to Him in such a way as to never be apart again. We invite Him into our innermost parts and He becomes our identity. We open up to Him, vulnerable and candid before Him, never hidden again. He enters and we are radically transformed into His likeness. We are forever loved, made new, married to God Himself.

"God, I invite you into the deepest part of me."
Soak in His presence and write down what He reveals.

# Day 21

SOS 3:6-11, *TPT*

*The Voice of the Lord*
*"Who is this one ascending from the wilderness in the pillar of*
*the glory cloud? He is fragrant with the anointing oils of myrrh*
*and frankincense—more fragrant than all the spices of the*
*merchant.*
*"Look! It is the king's marriage carriage. The love seat*
*surrounded by sixty champions, the mightiest of Israel's host, are*
*like pillars of protection.*
*"They are angelic warriors standing ready with swords to defend*
*the king and his fiancée from every terror of the night.*
*"The king made this mercy seat for himself out of the finest*
*wood that will not decay.*
*"Pillars of smoke, like silver mist—a canopy of golden glory*
*dwells above it. The place where they sit together is sprinkled*
*with crimson. Love and mercy cover this carriage, blanketing his*
*tabernacle throne. The king himself has made it for those who*
*will become his bride.*
*"Rise up, Zion maidens, brides-to-be! Come and feast your eyes*
*on this king as he passes in procession on his way to his*
*wedding. This is the day filled with overwhelming joy—the day*
*of his great gladness."*

The King comes in the "glory cloud," and is extravagantly fragrant with anointing oils, myrrh and frankincense. These two oils have incredible healing properties; just as when we enter into His healing presence, there is physical, emotional, and spiritual health in Him. His presence has an unmistakable, tangible effect on all who encounter Him, drawing us into His unparalleled aroma and great gladness.

The King is inviting His bride to join the marriage procession, to come into His presence, and great gladness that He has for you. And His love and mercy for you is unfailing, unwavering, never ceasing, and irrepressible. The mercy seat is fashioned in such a way that it won't decay, because He is the same yesterday, today, and forever. The wood does not decay as Jesus did not decay; this wood is not affected by outside influences. It has no death in it whatsoever. Because we are His body, we will never undergo decay; we become eternally living sons and daughters of God.

"But as many as received Him, to them He gave the right to become children of God, to those who believe in His name" (John 1:12, *NKJV*). We have the right to become His children. And John 3:16b, "whosoever believes in Him will not perish but have everlasting life" (*NKJV*). Whosoever. This invitation to become His bride is for all.

This can be your day of overwhelming joy. This is your day of breakthrough from the old into the new, a day of new beginnings, of a life full of joy, power, grace, mercy, and protection all in the Holy Spirit.

Being married to God is not a bunch of rules and regulations that no one can adhere to and continually keeps us in bondage. Being married to God creates a safe place where we are covered by gold, hidden in His redemption, seated in the chair named mercy, and sprinkled with His cleansing blood.

Catch His joy for you, His eagerness for his brides. You are His bride. You are His beloved. Lift up your head from life's daily toils and see your King turn His head to you and smile with joy, because you have looked His way.

"Today is my day of overwhelming joy! You are my safe place. Father, how do you see me?"

_____
_____
_____
_____
_____
_____
_____
_____
_____
_____
_____
_____
_____
_____
_____
_____
_____
_____
_____
_____
_____
_____
_____
_____
_____
_____
_____
_____
_____
_____
_____
_____
_____
_____
_____
_____
_____

# Day 22

SOS 3:7-10, *TPT*

*The Voice of the Lord*
*"Look! It is the king's marriage carriage. The love seat*
*surrounded by sixty champions, the mightiest of Israel's host, are*
*like pillars of protection.*
*"They are angelic warriors standing ready with swords to defend*
*the king and his fiancée from every terror of the night.*
*"The king made this mercy seat for himself out of the finest*
*wood that will not decay.*
*"Pillars of smoke, like silver mist—a canopy of golden glory*
*dwells above it. The place where they sit together is sprinkled*
*with crimson. Love and mercy cover this carriage, blanketing his*
*tabernacle throne. The king himself has made it for those who*
*will become his bride."*

This mercy seat is surrounded by sixty champion hosts, the mightiest pillars of protection. These pillars of protection are different than bars of a prison. God never puts us into bondage. He gives us a safe place of freedom.

A friend of mine in the military went to Iraqi during the early 2000's. While he was there, the military would make a protected playfield for those needing rest or recreation, especially for the children. It became a safe place in the midst of conflict where they played as if nothing could harm them.

There is freedom in protection. In Him, there is no fear, no hindrance, only freedom to love Him and to be relational. There is no fear in love. There is safety to be who He crafted us to be. If we make a mistake, we confess and repent, and let ourselves be transformed by renewing of our minds. We can be free to move past issues, without guilt or pity holding us back, and to press on to our higher call.

Jesus blood on the cross covers everything, every stain washed clean. With our new, divine nature, we overwhelmingly conquer according to Romans 8:37: "Yet even in the midst of all these things, we triumph over them all, for God has made us to be more than conquerors, and his demonstrated love is our glorious victory over everything!" (*TPT*). The "old man" is dead and doesn't need to be resurrected. Jesus lives in us and we live in

Him. Our new place is seated with Him in heavenly places as spoken of in Ephesians 1:20. We are seated with Him on His mercy seat carried by sixty warrior champion protectors. The number sixty means to uphold, help, or support—a firm foundation. Here we are seated with Him on the marriage seat that was skillfully crafted just for you and me, raised and carried on the foundation of protective pillars. And these warriors are no pacifists. They are actively protecting Jesus and His bride.

We are fully protected.

"Jesus, is there anything in my life holding me back from the new life you've given me?"

_____
_____
_____
_____
_____
_____
_____
_____
_____
_____
_____
_____
_____
_____
_____
_____
_____
_____
_____
_____
_____
_____
_____
_____
_____
_____
_____
_____
_____
_____
_____
_____
_____
_____

# Day 23

SOS 3:10, *TPT*

*The Voice of the Lord*
*"Pillars of smoke, like silver mist—a canopy of golden glory*
*dwells above it. The place where they sit together is sprinkled*
*with crimson. Love and mercy cover this carriage, blanketing his*
*tabernacle throne. The king himself has made it for those who*
*will become his bride."*

The pillars are like a silver mist and above it is a canopy of golden glory. The color silver speaks to redemption and gold to royalty and provision. They are hidden in His very presence. I know people who saw His "glory cloud." I've seen it in a few places and it reminded me of a mist. In Exodus 13:21 God came to the Israelites in a fire by night and a cloud by day. The end of Leviticus 9, a cloud of His glory fell so thick that the people shouted for joy and fell facedown. In 2 Chronicles 7:1-3, God's presence came so heavily the priests could not stand to minister.

At Azusa Street during the revival there was a mist that was almost always present about six inches off the ground. A number of times this mist would rise periodically during the revival, until flames would rise from the building and meet fire from the sky. Witnesses regularly called the LA fire department. Other witnesses testified that the cloud contained the purest air and the children played in it.

The silver smoke is like a burning sacrifice, in Old Testament times, was a sweet smelling aroma to God. In that culture, silver was the monetary exchange for an object or item to be redeemed or bought. We are of great value to God. We are hidden in His sacrifice.

We are covered together in His canopy of gold, of adornment and purity. Gold is also significant because its value increases as time passes. There are seven Hebrew words that refer to gold—seven is the number of perfection. His covering brings us to our original state He intended for us before the foundation of the world. Perfect.

Take a moment to seek Him, and then write down how He values you.

_____
_____
_____
_____
_____
_____
_____
_____
_____
_____
_____
_____
_____
_____
_____
_____
_____
_____
_____
_____
_____
_____
_____
_____
_____
_____
_____
_____
_____
_____
_____
_____
_____
_____

# Day 24

*The Bridegroom-King:*
*"Listen, my dearest darling, you are so beautiful—you are beauty itself to me! Your eyes glisten with love, like gentle doves behind your veil. What devotion I see each time I gaze upon you. You are like a sacrifice ready to be offered.*
*"When I look at you, I see how you have taken my fruit and tasted my word. Your life has become clean and pure, like a lamb washed and newly shorn. You now show grace and balance with truth on display.*
*"Your lips are as lovely as Rahab's scarlet ribbon, speaking mercy, speaking grace. The words of your mouth are as refreshing as an oasis. What pleasure you bring to me! I see your blushing cheeks opened like the halves of a pomegranate, showing through your veil of tender meekness.*
*"When I look at you, I see your inner strength, so stately and strong. You are as secure as David's fortress. Your virtues and grace cause a thousand famous soldiers to surrender to your beauty.*
*"Your pure faith and love rest over your heart as you nurture those who are yet infants."*

God is noticing you!

You are not invisible to Him. Not only is He noticing you, He sees every step you take, knows even the number of hairs on your head. You are beauty itself to Him. He says that you *have* become—not *will* become—pure and clean. He has every loving emotion each time He gazes on you, passion, longing. He is merciful, gracious, and forgiving, yet so holy.

He looks at you and sees royal strength and security. We are David's fortress. David was a worshiper; he worshiped whenever he needed security or strength.

"Your lips are as lovely as Rahab's scarlet ribbon," (Song of Songs 4:3, *TPT*). Rahab, in the book of Joshua, protected Israel's spies from the militia of Jericho, with that scarlet ribbon. By protecting those spies, she brought salvation to her family from the armies of Israel. She is in the genealogy of Jesus Who brought salvation and protection to a lost and dying world.

Let the words we speak to ourselves and to those we encounter be as refreshing as an oasis speaking mercy, grace, and love to others, words that bring pleasure to our heavenly Husband. Psalm 19:14a says, "Let the words of my mouth and the meditation of my heart be acceptable in Your sight" (*NKJV*).

The scarlet color of Rahab's ribbon represents the blood of Jesus that cleansed and freed us, gave us new life. The incomparable blood of Jesus covers us and He sees His sacrifice as lovely, which covers you. You are lovely.

Pure faith and love rest over our hearts as we nurture those He sends to us. We nurture them with words of life that come from hearts turned wholly toward Him.

"Bridegroom-King, I bring you great pleasure. Thank you for seeing me through Jesus' blood!"

"Does my mouth speak life every time I open it, and bring salvation and protection?"

_____

_____

_____

_____

_____

_____

_____

_____

_____

_____

_____

_____

_____

_____

_____

_____

_____

_____

_____

_____

_____

_____

_____

_____

_____

_____

_____

_____

_____

_____

_____

_____

_____

_____

_____

_____

_____

_____

_____

_____

_____

# Day 25

SOS 4:6, *TPT*

*The Shulamite:*
*"I've made up my mind. Until the darkness disappears and the dawn has fully come, in spite of shadows and fears, I will go to the mountaintop with you—the mountain of suffering love and the hill of burning incense. Yes, I will be your bride."*

The Creator of the universe wants us to go with Him up to the mountaintop. He wants our resounding yes. Become His bride. He invites us to marry the Creator of the universe!

If we're married, we (hopefully) care about our spouse's involvement and opinions of what we do and we communicate to help stay connected. Turning to Him any moment in our day keeps us connected. Run up that mountaintop with Him to a higher perspective, a better view of what is real—not to escape reality, but to see the truth. He invites us up to be with Him, to rule with Him, to love with Him.

He says in Genesis that the two become one flesh. When we become one with Him, we become kingdom beings, spirit people, because His DNA is inside us. He impregnates us with His image and we birth Jesus in what we live out daily.

In this verse, the Shulamite commits to being his bride. In order to become His bride we have to say yes to His proposal, yes to Him. This will cost us everything, but He is so worth the cost. We may not have anything to give Him but in exchange, He gives us His everything. Getting to our "yes" might not the easiest decision, it might even the most difficult for us to make, yet it's the most rewarding—to be face to face with God, never looking away, never turning back.

Are you ready to give Jesus your "yes?" If so, write as though you are signing a blank contract and God is going to fill it in.

If you're not ready, ask Him, "Father, what am I holding onto as more important than You?"

_____
_____
_____
_____
_____
_____
_____
_____
_____
_____
_____
_____
_____
_____
_____
_____
_____
_____
_____
_____
_____
_____
_____
_____
_____
_____
_____
_____
_____
_____
_____
_____
_____
_____

# Day 26

## SOS 4:7-8, *TPT*

*The Bridegroom-King:*
*"Every part of you is so beautiful, my darling. Perfect is your beauty, without flaw within.*
*"Now you are ready, my bride, to come with me as we climb the highest peaks together. Come with me through the archway of trust. We will look down from the crest of the glistening mounts and from the summit of our sublime sanctuary. Together we will wage war in the lion's den and the leopard's lair as they watch nightly for their prey."*

"Every part of you is so beautiful." This is how God sees you. You are lovely, without flaw, perfect. Your "yes" is perfect. He makes and molds you without spot or wrinkle.

After your "yes," you are ready for anything! Once we gave Him our yes He takes us away to the highest peaks. On the tallest peak we have a new, higher perspective, an eagles view, a kingdom view. We walk through the archway of trust—the Hebrew word for trust, *batach*, is where we get our word for amen, our "yes."

Freedom lies in trust. We come with Him through the archway looking down from that crest and see from this new perspective. From here, we can wage war on the predators below. Kingdom means the "king's domain," so freedom is the "domain of the free." Those whom He sets free are perfectly free. For the sake of freedom He sets us free—free *from* and free *to.* We are freed from sin and bondage and now free to love and to serve Jesus.

To God, you are without flaw. In this place of "yes" on the mountaintop, you are above life's struggles. From here you have all power.

"Jesus, what do you see happening and changing, in my circumstances for the good? Show me how to take authority and bring the kingdom into every area."

_____
_____
_____
_____
_____
_____
_____
_____
_____
_____
_____
_____
_____
_____
_____
_____
_____
_____
_____
_____
_____
_____
_____
_____
_____
_____
_____
_____
_____
_____
_____
_____
_____
_____

# Day 27

SOS 4:9-12, *TPT*

*The Bridegroom-King:*
*"For you reach into my heart. With one flash of your eyes I am*
*undone by your love, my beloved, my equal, my bride. You leave*
*me breathless—I am overcome by merely a glance from your*
*worshiping eyes, for you have stolen my heart. I am held hostage*
*by your love and by the graces of righteousness shining upon you.*
*"How satisfying to me, my equal, my bride. Your love is my*
*finest wine—intoxicating and thrilling. And your sweet,*
*perfumed praises—so exotic, so pleasing.*
*"Your loving words are like the honeycomb to me; your tongue*
*releases milk and honey, for I find the Promised Land flowing*
*within you. The fragrance of your worshiping love surrounds you*
*with scented robes of white.*
*"My darling bride, my private paradise, fastened to my heart. A*
*secret spring are you that no one else can have—my bubbling*
*fountain hidden from public view."*

Have you ever considered how you make Him feel?

Our "heavenly husband" can't contain Himself any longer and bursts out with how He feels deep inside for His loved one, for you. One glance from your eyes and He is undone, breathless, overcome. You have stolen His heart. He's so captivated by you that you hold Him hostage, and in you He is satisfied. You are His equal.

Your love thrills Him; it's intoxicating to Him. Your praises are a sweet, exotic aroma to Him. Your words are like milk and honey to Him, nourishing desert, the icing on the cake of who you are to Him. The fragrance of your loving worship surrounds you like a white robe or cloak, clean and spotless with a pure fragrance.

You are His personal paradise attached unrelentingly to His heart. You are perfect for Him.

He lavishes love on you, but He's also ravished by your love. He is swept away like a man caught in a tsunami wave of love, overwhelmed and overcome by you and your beauty.

"Lord, show me how You can truly say I am Your equal."

# Day 28

SOS 4:15, *TPT*

*The Bridegroom-King:*
*"Your life flows into mine, pure as a garden spring. A well of*
*living water springs up from within you, like a mountain brook*
*flowing into my heart!"*

Your life flows into His, pure as a garden spring, clear enough to drink as it feeds the surroundings. You nourish Him, God of all creation. This relationship is very much two sided, flowing both ways. We are often very aware of how we need Him and His love, and how we want to soak in the river of His presence. But did you know that you, too, are a well of living water flowing into His heart? You are so important to Him that He wants to soak in the river of your presence, too.

Rivers flow down from higher ground toward sea level. When we say "yes" to Him and give Him our all, we humble ourselves to sea level, and His river flows down over us. But in return, He does the same for us, by not removing our free will when we give Him our "yes," but partnering with us in what we do for Him and through Him. And His river flows through us to others. He welcomes the flow of our rivers into His heart.

"My life is a river of living water, flowing into Your heart, God. Reveal what this means to You, Lord."

# Day 29

## SOS 5:2-3, *TPT*

*The Shulamite Bride:*
*"After this I let my devotion slumber, but my heart for him*
*stayed awake. I had a dream. I dreamed of my beloved—he was*
*coming to me in the darkness of night. The melody of the man I*
*love awakened me. I heard his knock at my heart's door as he*
*pleaded with me:*
*The Bridegroom-King:*
*"Arise, my love. Open your heart, my darling, deeper still to me.*
*Will you receive me this dark night? There is no one else but*
*you, my friend, my equal. I need you this night to arise and come*
*be with me. You are my pure, loyal dove, a perfect partner for*
*me. My flawless one, will you arise? For my heaviness and tears*
*are more than I can bear. I have spent myself for you throughout*
*the dark night."*

"He is coming to me in the darkness of night." When times get hard, you are not alone—there is light at the end of the tunnel. Darkness lasts for a night, a season, and no more.

God promises, "I will never leave you nor forsake you" (Hebrews 13:5, *NKJV*). He is right here with us through it all. Our Bridegroom-King reveals the depth of Himself in our darkest times, embracing us and revealing His nature to us. His nature is not defined or limited by our situations, but is always good. He doesn't want us to suffer. He comes to you with His song and awakens your heart, asking you, "Arise, will you receive Me in the darkest night?" He gives His everything just to draw you near in the dark times, and it is there that He shines brighter. The Bridegroom-King spent the night in tears searching for His beloved, like the shepherd who left the ninety-nine in search of the one. You are the precious one that He will search through the night for until He has you tucked back into His arms.

Just as He is not defined by your circumstances, neither are you. The dark night does not make you dark inside. We are in this world, but not of it; we're from another planet so to speak—citizens of Heaven—and we are visitors here, bearing the light of truth and love.

It can be easier to believe for others' futures than for our own, but until we do, we can't fully trust Him. "'For I know the thoughts that I think toward you," says the Lord, "thoughts of peace and not of evil, to give you a future and a hope'" (Jeremiah 29:11, *NKJV*). God is love; He is good, and He is good to *you*. He loves *you!*

"Father, Jesus, Holy Spirit, show me where You are and what You're doing during my hardest times?"

# Day 30

SOS 5:3–6a, *TPT*

*The Shulamite Bride:*
*"I have already laid aside my own garments for you. How could
I take them up again since I've yielded my righteousness to
yours? You have cleansed my life and taken me so far. Isn't that
enough?*
*"My beloved reached into me to unlock my heart. The core of my
very being trembled at his touch. How my soul melted when he
spoke to me!*
*"My spirit arose to open for more of his touch. As I surrendered
to him, I began to sense his fragrance—the fragrance of his
suffering love! It was the sense of myrrh flowing all through me!*
*"I opened my soul to my beloved . . . "*

We've already laid aside our garments, our own good
works and self-righteousness for him. "Isn't that enough?" No!
"How my soul melted when he spoke to me!" (Song of Songs
5:4b, *TPT*).

"I want more of You, God!" And He longs to take You
deeper into His love.

Myrrh is found by cutting the tree, like the tree that was
cut into the cross which flows through us, washing out our old
man, filling us with His blood, and making us new.

He gave His all. How can we not give everything we are
for a greater capacity to contain Him? A dear friend of mine once
said that a glass is not full until it overflows. In the process of our
surrender, our hearts expand to receive even more of Him. He
unlocks our hearts and we tremble at His touch and melt at His
voice. When we come into a love-relationship with Jesus, we come
alive as He speaks. We open, then He gives us more; we open a
little more, and He fills us even more. God always wants to go
deeper, to satisfy us with more until our very being is enriched by
His love, and still give us more.

"I want more of You, God! What can I empty out of myself so I have more capacity to be filled by You?"

"Fill me, my Beloved!"

# Day 31

## SOS 5:6-8, *TPT*

*The Shulamite Bride:*
*"I opened my soul to my beloved, but suddenly he was gone!*
*And my heart was torn out in longing for him. I sought his*
*presence, his fragrance, but could not find him anywhere. I called*
*out for him, yet he did not answer me. I will arise and search for*
*him until I find him.*
*"As I walked throughout the city in search of him, the overseers*
*stopped me as they made their rounds. They beat me and bruised*
*me until I could take no more. They wounded me deeply and*
*removed their covering from me.*
*"Nevertheless, make me this promise, you brides-to-be: if you*
*find my beloved one, please tell him I endured all travails for*
*him."*

Suddenly her heart longed for Him and she sought Him. But man didn't help her. The overseers removed their protection from her, beat her, and left her for dead. But her only concern is finding her love. No matter what other people say or do to us, we keep our focus on Jesus. He is our passion and anything or anyone that does not stir us to go deeper in Jesus, we run past them to get to our Beloved.

Where is God in this season you're in?

Seasons change. If we look for Him where we've always found Him and He's not there, then He's moved, but not left us. During a time in our lives, we might only feel His presence during corporate worship, another only in our quiet time alone, yet another season, only when we serve and minister to others. Some seasons, are all fire and manifestation all the time, and some are quiet. The quiet ones are often when we actually go deeper in Him. When the seasons change, it doesn't mean He's gone away. He's still there. He'll never lead you anyplace He is not. It's a challenge for you to find Him and His presence in this season; where is He and what is He doing?

Only a small child plays hide-and-seek by always hiding in the same spot. Older, wiser children playing the game will know not to repeat the same hiding spot over and over. So it would be silly for the seeker to always expect to find the other older children

77

in the exact same spot every time. They would get bored and quit. Our life is never boring with Him.

Whatever season you're in, I challenge you to seek Him out with the tenacity the Shulamite does her beloved. No matter what obstacles come at her, she still seeks Him. We have the promise "seek and you will find" (Matthew 7:7). God wants you to find Him.

"God, where are You in this season of my life?"

# Day 32

SOS 5:9–10, *TPT*

*Brides-to-Be:*
*"What love is this? How could you continue to care so deeply for him? Isn't there another who could steal away your heart? We see now your beauty, more beautiful than all the others. What makes your beloved better than any other? What is it about him that makes you ask us to promise you this?"*
*The Shulamite Bride*
*"He alone is my beloved. He shines in dazzling splendor yet is still so approachable—without equal as he stands above all others, outstanding among ten thousand!"*

The brides-to-be can't understand her desire to still seek Him despite her difficulties. The ones, you and me, who love Him so intensely, will disregard the treatment of others in order to go after Jesus. Some won't understand our dogged pursuit.

And why does she persist? Because He alone is my Beloved! None other can come close to comparing to Him. She has seen the fullness of His love, the care in His eyes, and His gentle expression. His words have anointed her with flowing, healing oil. His hands hold the ultimate power but He never uses it in anger. She knows His fragrance, and nothing else will satisfy her but Him.

We love Him because we know beyond a shadow of a doubt that there is no one like Him. No one will satisfy us like He does. He floods us with holy desire, and we in turn fill Him with passion for us. His kisses are so sweet, His whispers of love. He is delightful in every way.

"Reveal to me Your beauty and splendor so I can be undone with awe of You."

# Day 33

## SOS 6:2-3, *TPT*

*The Shulamite Bride:*
*"My lover has gone down into his garden of delight, the place*
*where his spices grow, to feast with those pure in heart. I know*
*we shall find him there.*
*"He is within me—I am his garden of delight. I have him fully*
*and now he fully has me!"*

If you are ever in a place where you can't find Him, go deep inside yourself. He is there. He is always in His garden of delight, reveling in you.

"I have him fully and now he fully has me!" (Song of Songs 6:3b, *TPT*).

The brides-to-be have just witnessed her passion for her bridegroom-king. When others see our passion, our pursuit of our beloved, our zeal stirs them up to desire a deeper life. Being fully surrendered into His love is attractive.

We are the spices that bring flavor to foods that others eat. When He lives inside us we have Him fully, completely. We get all of Him. The Shulamite is excited in this place of full surrender. Kathryn Kuhlman said that it will cost us everything but it's worth it. She had nothing but her love to offer Him, and she gave Him everything, every part of herself.

Can you? What are you willing to surrender to find the Shulamite's delight?

"Lord, I give you everything. Show me how You delight in me."

# Day 34

SOS 6:4-9a, *TPT*

*The Bridegroom-King:*
*"O my beloved, you are lovely. When I see you in your beauty, I*
*see a radiant city where we will dwell as one. More pleasing than*
*any pleasure, more delightful than any delight, you have ravished*
*my heart, stealing away my strength to resist you. Even hosts of*
*angels stand in awe of you.*
*"Turn your eyes from me; I can't take it anymore! I can't resist*
*the passion of these eyes that I adore. Overpowered by a glance,*
*my ravished heart—undone. Held captive by your love, I am*
*truly overcome! For your undying devotion to me is the most*
*yielded sacrifice.*
*"The shining of your spirit shows how you have taken my truth*
*to become balanced and complete.*
*"Your beautiful blushing cheeks reveal how real your passion is*
*for me, even hidden behind your veil of humility.*
*"I could have chosen any from among the vast multitude of royal*
*ones who follow me. But one is my beloved dove . . . "*

Jesus is ravished by you! Your undying devotion, even
through all the hard times, is the most yielded sacrifice. He's
captivated by *your* love.

Your beauty reminds Him of a radiant city, rising and
shining as a beacon to the orphaned, unloved, and lonely. It shines
to draw those lost in closer, to release them from all that alienates.
You are more pleasing than any pleasure. You are more delightful
than any delight. You go exceedingly further into His heart than
anything. You satisfy Him beyond anything you can imagine.

Your spirit shines because you have taken to heart His
truth, which has made you balanced and complete. The nutrients
of His words go to every cell in your body and become your
strength. You are complete, the finished work of the master
craftsman, lacking no good thing. He says your cheeks are vibrant
with the passion you have for Him—it becomes obvious to those
around you. Even hidden beneath the veil of humility, it shows.

Humility is often mistaken for thinking less of yourself, a
negative perspective. True humility is knowing exactly who you
are in Him without exalting yourself. Let Him have the
opportunity to exalt you.

He could have chosen any one of 7.6 billion people, but He didn't. He chose you. He reached down and plucked you out of chaos and makes you to shine, prepares you for being a bride without spot or wrinkle. He prepares you to rule, to bring His kingdom to Earth. Once you take His "ring" you are His responsibility, His primary concern. Every day, He chooses you.

"Jesus, I open my heart to the depths of Your love. Show me the special way you adore me. Why did you choose me?"

# Day 35

SOS 6:9-10, *TPT*

*The Bridegroom-King:*
*"But one is my beloved dove—unrivaled in beauty, without*
*equal, beyond compare, the perfect one, the favorite one. Others*
*see your beauty and sing of your joy. Brides and queens chant*
*your praise: 'How blessed is she!'*
*"Look at you now—arising as the dayspring of the dawn, fair*
*as the shining moon. Bright and brilliant as the sun in all its*
*strength. Astonishing to behold as a majestic army waving*
*banners of victory."*

Yes, He chose you, His beloved dove with unrivaled beauty—without equal. You are perfect, His favorite. Others sing of your joy and chant how blessed you are—they're very aware of what you now carry.

Your past doesn't matter; it's been redeemed and restored. Look at you now! You arise like the dawn! There is no dawn if there hadn't once been night in your life. You are new creation because you're in Christ; you're powerful, healed, and free, a bright shining light. You aren't a patched up version of your old self, but a prototype that has never been.

We don't have the opportunity to witness the astonishing thrill of seeing our majestic armies waving banners of victory after we just won, joyful and cheering with loud, joined voices. You've won—when Christ died on the cross. In this realization, you now walk in joyful victory, and it's glorious to behold.

"Lord, show me what walking in joyous victory looks like in my life. Let me see through Your eyes, the results, the outcomes, the solutions to problems. I trust You with my tomorrows."

# Day 36

## SOS 6:11–12, *TPT*

*The Shulamite Bride:*
*"I decided to go down to the valley streams where the orchards of
the king grow and mature. I longed to know if hearts were
opening. Are the budding vines blooming with new growth? Has
their springtime of passionate love arrived?
"Then suddenly my longings transported me. My divine desire
brought me next to my beloved prince, sitting with him in his
royal chariot. We were lifted up together!"*

I decided.

At some point we must come to a place of "I decide" and
do it. Another "yes" to go deeper, more commitment, more
abandonment of self, and so much more joy. But this yes comes
from a "divine desire." She wants more. The Shulamite wants to
know if the springtime of their passionate love has arrived, and
her desire for more intimacy transports her to sitting with him in
his royal chariot, being lifted up together. This is a time of dreams
fulfilled.

Give Him your "yes." Let Him fill in the blanks. It will
cost you everything, but no one can take that away from you. In
return, He gives you His everything and you are lifted up with
Him.

"Yes, God. I give you my all! I want to know more of You. What dreams are yet to be fulfilled in my life and what does that look like from Your perspective?

_____

_____

_____

_____

_____

_____

_____

_____

_____

_____

_____

_____

_____

_____

_____

_____

_____

_____

_____

_____

_____

_____

_____

_____

_____

_____

_____

_____

_____

_____

_____

# Day 37

SOS 6:13-14, *TPT*

*Zion Maidens, Brides-to-Be:*
*"Come back! Return to us, O maiden of his majesty. Dance for*
*us as we gaze upon your beauty."*
*The Shulamite Bride:*
*"Why would you seek a mere Shulamite like me? Why would*
*you want to see my dance of love?"*
*The Bridegroom-King:*
*"Because you dance so gracefully, as though you dance with*
*angels!"*

Why would you want to see me?

He replies, "Because there is nothing that compares with you. What you bring to this world is so graceful, so heavenly, as though what you do for Me is a dance with angels." Your deepest dreams and desires fulfilled is a beautiful dance with the Creator that brings Heaven to earth. If you dance for Him, then dance, and know He approves. Whatever it is you're passionate about that you do for Him, He approves. He placed that desire in you, and He is excited to watch you flourish.

Words of affirmation, hugs, encouraging words are awesome and bring the Kingdom; everyone can do it. But she's discovering here, that there's more to her than she knew. She has a special gift, a talent. The beautiful product of you being you, is that His love flows off of you to everyone around. Your gifts and talents are conduits for His light to shine on people.

"God, what have you given me to do, and how can we do this together? Who are you blessing, or going to bless, through my gifts and talents?"

_____
_____
_____
_____
_____
_____
_____
_____
_____
_____
_____
_____
_____
_____
_____
_____
_____
_____
_____
_____
_____
_____
_____
_____
_____
_____
_____
_____
_____
_____
_____

# Day 38

SOS 7:1, *TPT*

*The Bridegroom-King:*
*"How beautiful on the mountains are the sandaled feet of this*
*one bringing such good news. You are truly royalty! The way you*
*walk so gracefully in my ways displays such dignity. You are*
*truly the poetry of God—his very handiwork."*

The graceful way you walk in God's ways will beautify any place you go. You watch God walk, and then you mirror Him, which is full of grace and beautifies everything. You display unsurpassed dignity in Jesus, a visible testament to His goodness.

You are the poetry of God! Poetry is an art form with words that takes time to carefully craft until the rhythm and sound rolls off the tongue to create a world of beauty. This is poetry, His masterpiece, His handiwork. You are the verse of God, voiced to a generation that will echo through time and eternity.

How then could we think ourselves anything less? Even our feet are beautiful!

Listen to creation itself, the earth, the sky; the sounds are so beautiful, birds' cheerful chirrups, babbling brooks, wind singing through trees on majestic mountains. And we are even more beautiful.

"What poetry are You speaking over me and about me?"

_____

_____

_____

_____

_____

_____

_____

_____

_____

_____

_____

_____

_____

_____

_____

_____

_____

_____

_____

_____

_____

_____

_____

_____

_____

_____

_____

_____

_____

_____

_____

_____

_____

_____

_____

_____

# Day 39

## SOS 7:2–3, *TPT*

*The Bridegroom-King:*
*"Out of your innermost being is flowing the fullness of my*
*Spirit—never failing to satisfy. Within your womb there is a*
*birthing of harvest wheat; they are the sons and daughters*
*nurtured by the purity you impart. How gracious you have*
*become!"*

Our innermost being is the very essence of who we are, and out of that part of us, flows the fullness of the Holy Spirit.

There is nothing stagnant about this flow. In John 7:38, Jesus said, "Believe in me so that rivers of living water will burst out from within you, flowing from your innermost being, just like the Scripture says!" (*TPT*).

You came thirsty for more, and you drink of Jesus; you drink the water that never fails to satisfy, water that is the fullness of His Spirit. His fullness is eternal, giving us infinite resources at our disposal and flowing out of us into a generation desperate for hope.

Our wombs, the creative part that produces fruit, are birthing a harvest. There comes a time in the actual birthing process when that baby won't stay in the womb. We are so full, we have to give what we have to others or we would burst. We nurture sons and daughters by the purity we impart. Everything we do is from this place of grace.

"Lord, show me the harvest I'm birthing."

# Day 40

SOS 7:4, *TPT*

*The Bridegroom-King:*
*"Your life stands tall as a tower, like a shining light on a hill.*
*Your revelation eyes are pure, like pools of refreshing—a*
*sparkling light for a multitude. Such discernment surrounds you,*
*protecting you from the enemy's advance."*

Let your life shine! In Matthew 5:15-16, Jesus talks about not lighting a lamp and placing it under a bushel, in a hidden place, but putting the light where everyone can use the light to see. Our light shines so that God would be glorified.

Your life shines like a tower of light on a hill. Lighthouses are positioned at the highest point of visibility to light the darkness so sailors can find their way and not crash onto the rocky shoal. You are a lighthouse on display, in a position to guide people to safety.

You reach more people with His love than you know. No one in Him can say he or she is an insignificant life just passing through history. You have a lasting effect on every life you encounter.

You see through eyes of revelation, bringing refreshing and truth to people, to a multitude. Revelation eyes see in the Spirit, gaining wisdom and discernment. They are pure like refreshing pools, ground of fertile thoughts that produce a harvest. The definition of discernment is the ability to judge well, to obtain sharp perceptions, and the ability to grasp and comprehend what is unseen; it is perception in the absence of judgment. This discernment forms a protective barrier from the enemy's advance. As a shining tower, you are quite visible, but fully protected.

"Lord, show me how I affect Your world."

# Day 41

SOS 7:5-6, *TPT*

*The Bridegroom-King:*
*"Redeeming love crowns you as royalty. Your thoughts are full of*
*life, wisdom, and virtue. Even a king is held captive by your*
*beauty.*
*"How delicious is your fair beauty; it can't be described as I*
*count the delights you bring to me. Love has become the*
*greatest."*

You are royalty, and redeeming love is your crown. Redeem means to recover ownership by paying a sum to fulfill a pledge; set free from slavery, to restore the honor, worth or reputation; to serve as compensation for, atone for. Redeeming love is given with no interest in having anything returned. Redemption fills in the gaps, lack of knowledge, character deficiencies. Paul talks about his own flaws, saying "And He said to me, 'My grace is sufficient for you, for My strength is made perfect in weakness'" (2 Corinthians 12:9, *NKJV*).

God lavishes His redeeming love on you, but it isn't a stagnant force. It flows out of you, because that's what royalty does in the Kingdom; the royal give away what is given to make space for even greater outpouring of His love. As this love flows out of you, people are affected even on a finite level, and you are actually changing and impacting history.

The King is held captive by your beauty; your thoughts are beautiful, full of life, wisdom, and virtue. Your beauty radiates from within, this indescribable, delicious quality that satisfies. You are satisfying. You are enough. Of all you bring to Him, love is supreme. "And now abide faith, hope, and love, these three; but the greatest of these is love" (1 Corinthians 13:13, *NKJV*) Regardless of what we do, think, or say, love is the most important and most powerful.

"My King, show me how I satisfy and captivate You."

# Day 42

SOS 7:7–9, *TPT*

*The Bridegroom-King:*
*"You stand in victory above the rest, stately and secure as you*
*share with me your vineyard of love.*
*"Now I decree, I will ascend and arise. I will take hold of you*
*with my power, possessing every part of my fruitful bride. Your*
*love I will drink as wine, and your words will be mine.*
*"For your kisses of love are exhilarating, more than any delight*
*I've known before. Your kisses of love awaken even the lips of*
*sleeping ones."*

Vineyards are carefully groomed, lovingly tended for the fruit they will bear. Yours is a vineyard of love having been nurtured and given all you need, a vineyard that has drunk up all the water, all the sunshine, and all the blessings. Now you stand strong and secure in victory, above the rest, like the lighthouse, not because of anything you've done, but by letting go and trusting Him with your needs, with removing the weed-obstacles that would threaten you, with blessing you with water and sunshine.

Now that you are so wholly partnered with Him He fills every single part of you. He is exhilarated by this union, this sweet surrender. And here you become His fruitful bride. And the more fruit you bear and give away, the more you will produce. In this process, He comes alive by your kisses of love and in this place with Him you can be confident that the words out of your mouth are His. Because of love. Because love is the greatest. Because it's not by works but by redeeming, loving salvation. The love you carry awakens others, stirs the parts of their hearts that are dead back to life, stirs hunger for more of Him.

Take a moment to experience His love for you and journal what He reveals.

Then ask Him for an encouraging word for someone in your life.

# Day 43

SOS 7:10-11, *TPT*

*The Shulamite Bride:*
*"Now I know that I am filled with my beloved and all his*
*desires are fulfilled in me.*
*"Come away, my lover. Come with me to the faraway fields. We*
*will run away together to the forgotten places and show them*
*redeeming love."*

You are not full until you overflow, like leaving a cup under the kitchen faucet even after it's full to the brim so that it spills over. Overflow happens when you *know* you are filled with Him, and that His desires, too, are fulfilled in you. Then this love leaks out of you onto everyone around you, waking up the forgotten places with this incredible love.

When we awaken and stir God we become totally aware of Him filling us. It is tangible, unforgettable, to know all His desires are satisfied in us. What is this indescribable passion He pours on us? To be the object of His every desire! He has an insatiable appetite for us, and yet all His desires are fulfilled in us.

With this love brimming, spilling over from our hearts, we echo Jesus' cry to the forgotten places, to come away, to find Love. Just as earlier Jesus called us away from the fields to show *us* redeeming love, now we too can bring it to others. In the refreshment of His love, our fields and forgotten places become fulfilled. So hand in hand we run together to forgotten, abandoned, orphaned places to show, not just tell, them of redeeming love. This love buys them back, pays the price for them, and He can pour His love in them the same as He has done for us.

"Overflow me with Your love, God. If there is even one thing hindering this outpouring, show me what it is so we can remove it, because I want to be so filled with You, that I become more than an overflowing cup. I want to become a tsunami of Your love."

# Day 44

## SOS 7:12-13, *TPT*

*The Shulamite Bride:*
*"Let us arise and run to the vineyards of your people and see if the budding vines of love are now in full bloom. We will discover if their passion is awakened. There I will display my love for you.*
*The love apples are in bloom, sending forth their fragrance of spring. The rarest of fruits are found at our doors—the new as well as the old. I have stored them for you, my lover-friend!"*

Have you ever felt so much love for someone that you want to show that person off to everyone you know? The bride wants to run to her bridegroom's people and express to them how much she loves this man. She is overflowing with her passion for him.

It's out of a place of intimacy that we arise, not out of duty, but out of love for each other, in that place of love when you can say "I am His and He is mine." You now can "Arise, shine; for your light is come," as in Isaiah 60:1 (*NKJV*). Scientists have captured the flash of light occurring at the moment of conception from the fertilized egg. We shine as He impregnates us with the fertilized egg of God's handiwork that starts the process of birthing in us the *destiny* and *purpose* for which we were created.

Let us run to His vineyard to see if the budding flowers of love are in bloom. Jesus longs to plant in us love that germinates until His vineyard blooms. When we bloom, everyone can scent our love for Him and for others. We send forth the very fragrance of spring, where the Earth is filled with hope, new life, blossoming with intense beauty.

"Lover-Friend, am I blooming with the fullness of Your love right now?"

# Day 45

## SOS 8:1-3, *TPT*

*The Shulamite Bride:*
*"If only I could show everyone this passionate desire I have for you. If only I could express it fully, no matter who was watching me, without shame or embarrassment.*
*"I long to bring you to my innermost chamber—this holy sanctuary you have formed within me. O that I might carry you within me. I would give you the spiced wine of my love, this full cup of bliss that we share. We would drink our fill until...*
*"His left hand cradles my head while his right hand holds me close. We are at rest in this love."*

The Shulamite is so in love with her new Husband that she will express herself unashamedly. David was so overcome by his joy that he stripped down to his loincloth and danced for God through the streets. Many times I have been so overwhelmed that I could not fully or properly explore what was going on inside my spirit. Thank God for heaven's language that fills the gaps of this earthly one. We all need times where we fully express our passionate desire for God, putting all inhibitions aside and "let loose" in freedom. Even shouting, "I love you God!" can feel like a huge risk, but when we're so intoxicated with His love it no longer matters what others might be thinking.

As much as we desire to have Jesus come into our innermost intimate place, that holy refuge, He desires this even more—that we would share the drink of spiced wine of our love until He cradles our head with His left hand and holds us close with His right. This is the position of deep intimacy between a man and woman. It is also the way we hold a baby in care and love. Proverbs 3:16 talks about Him having long life is in His right hand and riches and honor is in His left. It is in this place of trust that we get our identity. Here, the shadow of God resides, the foundation of love, flowing both to Him and from Him. Drink in this love until trust brings you into rest.

107

Jesus says, "I am here. Come into my arms and let me love you like you've never been loved before."

_____
_____
_____
_____
_____
_____
_____
_____
_____
_____
_____
_____
_____
_____
_____
_____
_____
_____
_____
_____
_____
_____
_____
_____
_____
_____
_____
_____
_____
_____
_____
_____
_____

# Day 46

SOS 8:5, *TPT*

*The Bridegroom-King:*
*"Who is this one? Look at her now! She arises out of her desert,*
*clinging to her beloved. When I awakened you under the apple*
*tree, as you were feasting upon me, I awakened your innermost*
*being with the travail of birth as you longed for more of me."*

Remember that desert you rose out of? God can hardly recognize you now that you are so alive. If a desert wind tries to blow over your life, you arise, clinging to your beloved, because you know what you have in Him! You've already been awakened into love. You've tasted, feasted, and seen that the Lord is definitely good! You've tasted and longed for more and more even when you felt you couldn't take anymore. And now, because of this love, you look different. You look like one who has fallen head over heals in love for the God of the universe.

Love pumps through your veins. It's the very rhythm of your heart—the very rhythm of His heart. Deserts don't even look the same from this place of intimacy, of confidence in God's great love. Who would be afraid to walk through a desert now, knowing the God of the universe walks beside, carrying every imaginable supply—water, food, shelter…love. You walk like one of confidence, head held high, because you trust your God, your Lover and Friend, because your innermost being is awakened with the strength of birth as you long for more of Him. More of His goodness. More of His love. More presence. Nothing else matters but Him, your life-blood.

"I want more of You! Take me deeper into Your heart of love!"

_____
_____
_____
_____
_____
_____
_____
_____
_____
_____
_____
_____
_____
_____
_____
_____
_____
_____
_____
_____
_____
_____
_____
_____
_____
_____
_____
_____
_____

# Day 47

SOS 8:6-7, *TPT*

*The Bridegroom-King:*
*"Fasten me upon your heart as a seal of fire forevermore. This living, consuming flame will seal you as my prisoner of love. My passion is stronger than the chains of death and the grave, all consuming as the very flashes of fire from the burning heart of God. Place this fierce, unrelenting fire over your entire being. "Rivers of pain and persecution will never extinguish this flame. Endless floods will be unable to quench this raging fire that burns within you. Everything will be consumed. It will stop at nothing as you yield everything to this furious fire until it won't even seem to you like a sacrifice anymore."*

Fastening Him upon our hearts is a choice, born out of our desire for intimacy. As we long for more of Him, we attach Him to our hearts as a "fire seal" forevermore. This all-consuming fire seals us as prisoners of love, not locked away, but tied to Him with eternal bonds of love, forever keeping us close to Him.

His burning passion is stronger than anything the enemy can throw at us, originating from the very heart of God and consuming us fully. As we take possession of His passion, this fierce unrelenting fire, it no longer feels like a sacrifice, but an outpouring of love. We allow everything to be consumed in this furious fire just as Elijah's altar was consumed by the fire of God. Nothing can extinguish this flame as it burns deep within us. Nothing can separate us from His love.

"I choose to become a prisoner of Your love. I want the seal of fire burning with passion upon my heart. Take me deeper."

Recommended listening: "All Consuming Fire" and "Come Away" by Jesus Culture.

# Day 48

SOS 8:8-10, *TPT*

*The Shulamite Bride:*
*"My brothers said to me when I was young, 'Our sister is so immature. What will we do to guard her for her wedding day?'"*
*The Bridegroom-King:*
*"We will build a tower of redemption to protect her. Since she is vulnerable, we will enclose her with a wall of cedar boards."*
*The Shulamite Bride:*
*"But now I have grown and become a bride, and my love for him has made me a tower of passion and contentment for my beloved. I am now a firm wall of protection for others, guarding them from harm. This is how he sees me—I am the one who brings him bliss, finding favor in his eyes."*

We can look back on our life, how far we've come in the Lord. Even when we weren't looking for it, His protection was there—even in the times when it seems He wasn't, He was there. When we were new in the Lord and vulnerable, He enclosed us in walls of cedar boards. Cedar is known for its fragrant wood, but less known is its protective qualities as a bug repellent and its strong resistance to mold.

Now we've grown, and are growing still, into this tower of passion and contentment, a firm wall of protection for others. We become family to the newborns in Jesus, and we guard them and protect their innocence.

We know now that He sees us as the ones who bring Him bliss! We find favor in His eyes! Bliss is perfect happiness and great joy, typically so as to be oblivious to everything else—utter joy or contentment, wedded bliss, and the joy of heart. This is what we bring to God's heart.

"God, show me how I affect Your heart."

# Day 49

SOS 8:11-14, *TPT*

*The Shulamite Bride:*
*"My bridegroom-king has a vineyard of love made from a*
*multitude of followers. His caretakers of this vineyard have given*
*my beloved their best.*
*"But as for my own vineyard of love, I give it all to you forever.*
*And I will give double honor to those who serve my beloved and*
*have watched over my soul.*
*"My beloved, one with me in my garden, how marvelous that my*
*friends, the brides-to-be, now hear your voice and song. Let me*
*now hear it again."*
*The Bridegroom-King to the Bride in a Divine Duet:*
**"Arise, my darling!**
*Come quickly, my beloved.*
**Come and be the graceful gazelle with me.**
*Come be like a dancing deer with me.*
**We will dance in the high place of the sky,**
*yes, on the mountains of fragrant spice.*
**Forever we shall be united as one!"**

The reward of total surrender—He gives us His all, too.

Oh, to be in divine duet with my Bridegroom-King! I give it all to you forever!

We are one, He and I, you and He, in the garden. How marvelous that the brides-to-be, that others, can now hear the voice of the Lord, can hear His song of love pouring from His heart.

The presence of Holy Spirit, having Him love others through us is worth the cost. Even if all you have is love for Him, give it all to Him.

In our surrender, Jesus opens the floodgates of Heaven. In our surrender, He commissions us to arise, to take our place, to come and be. Not try, but simply get up and come. Don't act or strive, just come and be. Dance! Jesus wants to dance in joy with us in our journey, "We will dance in the high place . . . " We dance out of ecstasy that His presence has come home to us. The wedding dance as David did uninhibited, unashamedly, and with all gusto. The dance of total, sweet surrender.

"My Bridegroom-King, I give you everything I have and all that I am. Dance with me!"

Suggested listening: "Dance with Me" by Jesus Culture.

_____
_____
_____
_____
_____
_____
_____
_____
_____
_____
_____
_____
_____
_____
_____
_____
_____
_____
_____
_____
_____
_____
_____
_____
_____
_____
_____
_____
_____
_____
_____
_____

# Day 50

SOS 7:1, *TPT*

*The Bridegroom-King:*
*"How beautiful on the mountains are the sandaled feet of this*
*one bringing such good news. You are truly royalty! The way you*
*walk so gracefully in my ways displays such dignity. You are*
*truly the poetry of God—his very handiwork."*

Imagine, now that you have finished the Song of Songs, that you have woken up from a dream where Jesus came to you and spoke the words of this verse directly to you. Because He has.

He approves of you. He more than accepts you. You are more than enough, because He doesn't see any shortcomings. They aren't visible through the covering of Jesus' blood. You are whiter than the freshest snow, purified. Because of His sacrifice, you can stand next to Jesus at the thrown of the Father, appearing as Jesus does, glorified and purified. You are truly royalty! You are His handiwork!

Go back to SOS 5:10-16 (*TPT*) where the Shulamite tells the brides-to-be why there is none like her beloved, and read it as a poem from your heart about Jesus.

Then read Jesus' answer to you again in SOS 7:1 (*TPT*).

Lord of lords, King of kings, I ask a special covering for my friend who has read this book, that You nurture and hold Your dear one close. Protect Your beloved from harm, covered and aware of the purest love You give, every moment of every day for the rest of my friend's life. In Jesus' name, amen!

Made in USA - Crawfordsville, IN
60260_9781948754002
11.14.2022 1146